BIOGRAPHY OF MARY EARPS

The Guardian of the Net

Ramon M.Jones

Mary Earps

All rights reserved. No part of this book may be reproduced, distributed, or transmitted in any form or by any means, including photocopying, recording, or other electronic or mechanical methods, without the prior written permission of the publisher, except in the case of brief quotations embodied in critical reviews and specific other noncommercial uses permitted by copyright law

Copyright @ **Michael P. Powell** 2024

Mary Earps

TABLE OF CONTENTS
INTRODUCTION
CHAPTER 1: WHO IS MARY EARPS?
CHAPTER 2: EARLY YEARS AND FAMILY BACKGROUND
CHAPTER 3: FIRST STEP IN FOOTBALL
CHAPTER 4: RISING THROUGH THE RANKS
CHAPTER 5; BECOMING A PROFESSIONAL
CHAPTER 6: HER TIME IN MANCHESTER UNITED

CHAPTER 7: INTERNATIONAL STARDOM
CHAPTER 8: ACHIEVEMENTS AND AWARDS
CHAPTER 9: HER GOALKEEPING SKILLS
CHAPTER 10: CHALLENGES AND HOW SHE OVERCAME
CHAPTER 12: IMPACT AND INSPIRING THE NEXT GENERATION
CONCLUSION

Mary Earps

INTRODUCTION

Hey there, young soccer fans! Are you ready to dive into the thrilling world of football and meet a real-life hero on the field? Join us on an exciting journey through the inspiring football career of Mary Earps, a resilient and talented goalkeeper who has proven that determination and hard work can lead to success. In this engaging book designed for kids, we will explore Mary's courageous journey from aspiring player to a goalkeeping guardian.Imagine a player who stands tall between the goalposts, fearlessly blocking shots and leading her team with confidence – that's Mary Earps. With her exceptional goalkeeping skills, sharp reflexes, and unwavering dedication, Mary has become a role model for young athletes aspiring to excel in the beautiful game.Through Mary's eyes, we

Mary Earps

will witness the thrills and challenges of being a goalkeeper, the importance of teamwork, and the power of never giving up on your dreams. Her story will inspire young readers to believe in themselves, work hard, and face adversity with courage and resilience.As you turn the pages of this book, get ready to be amazed by Mary Earps' bravery on the field and her passion for the game. Her journey highlights the values of teamwork, sportsmanship, and perseverance, showing that with determination and a positive attitude, anything is possible in soccer and in life.SO, lace up your boots, grab your gloves, and join us on this extraordinary adventure with Mary Earps as our guiding goalkeeper. Are you prepared to make heroic saves, defend your goal with courage, and chase your dreams with the same determination as this remarkable athlete? The soccer pitch awaits – let's kick off an

Mary Earps

unforgettable journey with Mary Earps as our fearless leader!

CHAPTER 1: WHO IS MARY EARPS?

Hey there, young soccer enthusiasts! Let's explore the exciting world of football and get to know a remarkable goalkeeper who is a true hero on the field – Mary Earps. Mary is not just any ordinary player; she is a fearless and talented athlete who has made a name for herself as a goalkeeping guardian, protecting her team's goal with determination and skill. Mary Earps is known for her bravery, quick reflexes, and unwavering dedication to her position as a goalkeeper. From diving to make spectacular saves to leading her team with confidence, Mary's passion for the game shines through in every match she plays.

But why is Mary Earps so special for kids, Well, she teaches us important lessons about courage, teamwork, and facing challenges head-on. Mary shows us that with hard work,

Mary Earps

practice, and a positive attitude, we can overcome obstacles and achieve our goals, both on and off the soccer field.

Watching Mary in action is like witnessing a real-life superhero defend her goal with strength and determination. With her inspiring leadership and never-give-up attitude, Mary is a role model for young athletes who dream of protecting the goal and making a difference for their team.

So, get ready to join Mary Earps on her soccer journey and be inspired to embrace challenges with courage and perseverance. Who knows, maybe one day you'll be out on the field, making heroic saves and leading your team to victory, just like the fearless Mary Earps. The soccer pitch is calling – let's defend our goals and chase our dreams with the spirit of a true goalkeeping guardian!

CHAPTER 2: EARLY YEARS AND FAMILY BACKGROUND

Mary Earps was born on March 7, 1993, in West Bromwich, England. She grew up in a football-loving family. Her father, Mark Earps, was a former professional footballer, and her mother, Julie Earps, played football for Aston Villa. Mary's two brothers, Jack and Lewis, are also involved in sports. Jack is a professional footballer, and Lewis is a professional rugby player.

Mary Earps started playing football at a young age. She joined the Birmingham City Ladies Centre of Excellence at the age of eight and played for the club's youth teams until she was 16. In 2009, she joined the England national team setup and has represented her country at various age levels.

Mary Earps

Mary Earps is a talented goalkeeper and has played for several professional clubs, including Birmingham City, Wolverhampton Wanderers, Reading, and Manchester City. She is currently the first-choice goalkeeper for the England national team and helped the team win the UEFA Women's Euro 2022 tournament.

Mary Earps is a role model for young girls and women who want to play football.

Mary Earps is a talented goalkeeper who has represented England at various age levels. She is currently the first-choice goalkeeper for the England national team and helped the team win the UEFA Women's Euro 2022 tournament. Earps is a role model for young girls and women who want to play football. She is a hard-working and dedicated player who has achieved great success in her career.

Earps started playing football at a young age. She joined the Birmingham City Ladies Centre

Mary Earps

of Excellence at the age of eight and played for the club's youth teams until she was 16. In 2009, she joined the England national team setup and has represented her country at various age levels. Earps is a talented goalkeeper who has played for several professional clubs, including Birmingham City, Wolverhampton Wanderers, Reading, and Manchester City. She is currently the first-choice goalkeeper for the England national team and helped the team win the UEFA Women's Euro 2022 tournament.

Earps is a role model for young girls and women who want to play football. Earps is a talented goalkeeper who has represented England at various age levels. She is currently the first-choice goalkeeper for the England national team and helped the team win the UEFA Women's Euro 2022 tournament.

CHAPTER 3:FIRST STEP IN FOOTBALL

Mary Earps started playing football at a young age. She joined the Birmingham City Ladies Centre of Excellence at the age of eight and played for the club's youth teams until she was 16. In 2009, she joined the England national team setup and has represented her country at various age levels.

Mary Earps is a talented goalkeeper and has played for several professional clubs, including Birmingham City, Wolverhampton Wanderers, Reading, and Manchester City. She is currently the first-choice goalkeeper for the England national team and helped the team win the UEFA Women's Euro 2022 tournament.

Mary Earps is a role model for young girls and women who want to play football. She is a hard-working and dedicated player who has achieved great success in her career.

Mary Earps

Mary Earps is a talented goalkeeper who has represented England at various age levels. She is currently the first-choice goalkeeper for the England national team and helped the team win the UEFA Women's Euro 2022 tournament. Earps is a role model for young girls and women who want to play football. She is a hard-working and dedicated player who has achieved great success in her career

CHAPTER 4:RISING THROUGH THE RANKS

Mary Earps's Journey: From Leicester to Doncaster

After leaving Birmingham City, Mary Earps continued to hone her skills at other clubs. She played for Leicester City and Nottingham Forest, gaining valuable experience and honing her abilities as a goalkeeper.

Leicester City provided Earps with a competitive environment where she could test her skills against talented players. She quickly established herself as a reliable goalkeeper and made impressive saves, earning the respect of her teammates and coaches.

Nottingham Forest offered Earps another opportunity to showcase her talent and further develop her game. During her time at

Mary Earps

Nottingham Forest, she faced a variety of challenges and learned how to adapt to different playing styles. Her experiences at both Leicester City and Nottingham Forest were instrumental in her growth as a goalkeeper. Doncaster Rovers Belles was the next stop in her journey. This club provided Earps with a platform to showcase her talent and further develop her skills. Her time at Doncaster Rovers Belles was crucial in her rise through the ranks of women's football. She played a key role in the team's success and made a name for herself as one of the most promising young goalkeepers in England.

Earps's journey from Leicester to Doncaster was an important step in her career. Her experiences at these clubs helped her to develop her skills and prepare for the challenges that lay ahead.

CHAPTER 5;BECOMING A PROFESSIONAL

Mary Earps's journey to becoming a professional footballer was marked by her impressive performances and dedication to her craft. After her time at Doncaster Rovers Belles, she returned to Birmingham City where she had started her youth career. This homecoming provided Earps with a familiar environment and an opportunity to contribute to the club's success.

Her performances at Birmingham City caught the attention of scouts from other clubs, and she eventually joined the Bristol Academy. This move allowed Earps to further develop her skills and compete at a higher level. She quickly became a key player for the Bristol

Academy and made a significant impact on the team's success.

Earps's impressive performances earned her a move to VfL Wolfsburg in the German Bundesliga. This was a major step in her career, as the Bundesliga is one of the top women's football leagues in the world. Earps faced stiff competition from talented goalkeepers but quickly established herself as a reliable and consistent performer.

Her time at VfL Wolfsburg was a valuable learning experience. She faced a variety of challenges, including adapting to a new language and culture, and learned how to adapt to different playing styles. Earps also had the opportunity to compete against some of the best players in the world, which helped her to improve her skills and raise her game.

One of the most notable aspects of Earps's time at VfL Wolfsburg was her ability to handle

Mary Earps

the pressure of playing for a top club in a highly competitive league. She consistently performed at a high level, even in big matches, and became a trusted and respected member of the team.
Earps's journey from Birmingham City to VfL Wolfsburg was a testament to her talent, hard work, and determination. Her experiences at these clubs helped her to develop into a world-class goalkeeper and prepare for the challenges that lay ahead.

Mary Earps

CHAPTER 6: HER TIME IN MANCHESTER UNITED

Mary Earps's journey continued to soar when she joined Manchester United in 2019. She quickly established herself as a key player for the Red Devils, bringing her exceptional goalkeeping skills and leadership qualities to the team.

Earps's presence between the sticks provided a solid foundation for Manchester United's defense. Her ability to command her area, make crucial saves, and distribute the ball accurately made her an invaluable asset to the team. She consistently performed at a high level, earning the respect and admiration of her teammates and fans.

One of Earps's most memorable moments at Manchester United came in the 2021-2022

Mary Earps

season when she made a crucial save to help her team defeat Chelsea in the FA Cup final. With the match tied and Chelsea pressing for a winner, Earps made a stunning save to deny a Chelsea striker and preserve the clean sheet. Her save sparked wild celebrations from the Manchester United fans and secured the team's victory, earning her widespread praise and recognition.

Earps's exceptional performances also contributed to Manchester United's success in the Women's Super League. She played a key role in the team's impressive run and helped them to secure a place in the top three of the league. Her ability to consistently deliver top-class performances made Earps a fan favorite at Manchester United. Her dedication, work ethic, and positive attitude made her a role model for young aspiring goalkeepers.

Mary Earps

Earps's time at Manchester United was a period of great success and personal growth. Her contributions to the team helped to elevate Manchester United's status in women's football and inspired a new generation of fans. She became a symbol of excellence and a role model for young girls and women who aspired to play football at the highest level.

Earps's journey at Manchester United was not without its challenges. She faced stiff competition from talented goalkeepers and had to adapt to the demands of playing for a top club in a highly competitive league. However, she never wavered in her determination and always gave her best on the field.

Her hard work and dedication paid off, and she became a key figure in Manchester United's success. She helped the team to win the FA Cup and secure a place in the top three of the Women's Super League. Her performances also earned her a place in the England national team, where she continued to excel.

Earps's time at Manchester United was a remarkable chapter in her career. She made a significant impact on the team and helped to inspire a new generation of fans. Her legacy at Manchester United will continue to be remembered for years to come.

CHAPTER 7: INTERNATIONAL STARDOM

Mary Earps has been a standout performer for the England national team, representing her country at various age levels. She has consistently impressed with her exceptional goalkeeping skills and her ability to handle pressure.

Earps's journey with the England national team began at a young age when she represented her country at the under-17 level. Her impressive performances earned her a call-up to the senior team, where she quickly established herself as a reliable and consistent goalkeeper.

Earps played a crucial role in England's success at the 2023 FIFA Women's World Cup. She was named the vice-captain of the team and her leadership qualities were evident throughout the tournament. Earps made several crucial saves, helping England to reach the final where they faced Spain.

Although England narrowly lost the final, Earps's performances earned her widespread praise and recognition. She was named the Best FIFA Women's Goalkeeper for her outstanding contributions to the England national team.

Earps's international stardom is a testament to her talent, hard work, and dedication. She has become a role model for young aspiring goalkeepers and has inspired a new generation of fans. Her journey from a young player to a world-class goalkeeper is an inspiration to many.

Earps's international career is still ongoing, and she continues to be a vital member of the England national team. Her exceptional

Mary Earps

goalkeeping skills and her leadership qualities make her a valuable asset to the team. As she continues to grow and develop, Earps is sure to achieve even greater success in the years to come.

CHAPTER 8:ACHIEVEMENTS AND AWARDS

Mary Earps has won numerous awards and recognitions throughout her career. She has been praised for her exceptional goalkeeping skills and her contributions to both club and country.

One of Earps's most notable achievements was winning the Golden Glove at the 2022 UEFA Women's Euro tournament. This award is given to the best goalkeeper in the tournament and is a testament to Earps's outstanding performances.

In addition to the Golden Glove, Earps has also been recognized for her contributions to Manchester United. She has been named the Manchester United Women's Player of the Year on several occasions and has been praised for her leadership qualities and her ability to inspire her teammates.

Earps has also been honored for her work with the England national team. She has been named the Best FIFA Women's Goalkeeper and has been recognized for her contributions to the team's success.

Other Honors and Recognitions

UEFA Women's Euro 2022 Champion

WSL Team of the Year

Manchester United Women's Player of the Year

PFA Players' Player of the Year

FSF Women's Player of the Year

FIFPro Women's World XI

Earps's awards and achievements are a testament to her talent, hard work, and dedication. She has become one of the most respected goalkeepers in women's football and

Mary Earps

has inspired a new generation of young girls to take up the sport.

CHAPTER 9:HER GOALKEEPING SKILLS

Mary Earps is a talented goalkeeper known for her exceptional skills and technical abilities.

Reflexes and Agility: Earps possess lightning-fast reflexes and agility, allowing her to react quickly to shots and make difficult saves. Her ability to move swiftly and change direction is a major asset.

Shot-Stopping: Earps is a master at shot-stopping. She has a strong command of her area and can make acrobatic saves to deny opponents. Her ability to anticipate shots and position herself correctly is a key factor in her success.

Handling: Earps is comfortable handling the ball with both hands and feet. She is confident in her ability to catch crosses and distribute the

ball accurately. Her handling skills are crucial for starting attacks from the back.
Communication: Earps is an excellent communicator and is always talking to her defenders to organize the defense and prevent goals. Her ability to direct her teammates and make crucial calls is a vital aspect of her game.
Mental Fortitude: Earps have a strong mental fortitude and is able to remain calm and focused under pressure. She is not afraid to make mistakes and is always looking to learn and improve.

Earps's Technical Abilities

In addition to her natural athleticism, Earps possesses excellent technical skills. She is comfortable using both hands and feet to handle the ball and is able to distribute the ball accurately to her teammates. Her ability to play out from the back and start attacks is a valuable asset to her team.

Mary Earps

Earps is also skilled at handling crosses and set pieces. She is confident in her ability to catch the ball under pressure and distribute it to her teammates. Her technical skills allow her to play a key role in her team's defensive and offensive strategies.

Mary Earps

CHAPTER 10:CHALLENGES AND HOW SHE OVERCAME

Mary Earps, like any successful athlete, has faced her fair share of challenges throughout her career. However, her determination and resilience have helped her overcome these obstacles and achieve great things.

Breaking into the Professional Game: As a young woman, Earps faced challenges in breaking into the professional game. Women's football was not as prominent as it is today, and there were fewer opportunities for female players to showcase their talent. However, Earps's hard work and dedication eventually paid off, and she was able to secure a professional contract with Birmingham City.

Injuries: Injuries are a common challenge for athletes, and Earps has not been immune to them. She has had to deal with injuries throughout her career, which have sidelined her for periods of time. However, Earps has always approached her recovery with a positive attitude and has worked hard to get back to full fitness.

Pressure and Expectations: As a highly talented goalkeeper, Earps has faced immense pressure and expectations. She has been expected to perform at the highest level and has often been under the spotlight. However, Earps has handled this pressure with maturity and has consistently delivered impressive performances.

Stereotypes and Discrimination: Women's football has faced stereotypes and discrimination in the past. Earps has had to deal with negative perceptions about women's sports and has faced challenges in gaining recognition for her achievements. However, she has remained focused on her goals and has used her platform to challenge stereotypes and promote gender equality.

How Earps Overcame Her Challenges

Mary Earps has overcome her challenges through her determination, resilience, and hard work. She has never given up on her dreams, even when faced with setbacks. Earps has also benefited from the support of her family, friends, and teammates, who have encouraged her to pursue her goals.

Earps's positive attitude and mental toughness have also been key factors in her success. She has learned to handle pressure and adversity and has always remained focused on her goals. Her ability to bounce back from setbacks and learn from her mistakes has been crucial in her development as a player.

Earps's commitment to social justice has also been a source of strength. She has used her

Mary Earps

platform to challenge stereotypes and promote gender equality. Her advocacy for women's rights has helped to create a more inclusive and equitable environment for female athletes. Mary Earps's journey is a testament to the power of determination, resilience, and hard work. She has overcome significant challenges to become one of the best goalkeepers in the world. Her story is an inspiration to young girls and women who want to pursue their dreams, no matter what obstacles they may face.

CHAPTER 11: HER LIFE OFF THE COURT

While Mary Earps is a world-class goalkeeper, she is also a well-rounded individual with a variety of interests and hobbies. Off the field, Earps enjoys spending time with her family and friends, exploring new places, and giving back to the community.

Mary's Interests and Hobbies

Traveling: Earps loves to travel and explore new places. She enjoys experiencing different cultures and trying new things. Her travels have taken her to various destinations around the world, including Europe, Asia, and North America. She is always looking for new adventures and opportunities to broaden her horizons.

Mary Earps

Music: Earps is a music enthusiast and enjoys listening to a variety of genres. She is often seen attending concerts and festivals, and she has a particular fondness for indie rock and alternative music. Earps's love of music is evident in her social media posts, where she often shares her favorite songs and artists.

Fashion: Earps has a keen interest in fashion and is often seen sporting stylish outfits on and off the field. She is known for her bold and colorful style, and she is often seen experimenting with different trends. Earps's fashion sense has earned her a following on social media, where she shares her outfits and style tips.

Reading: Earps is a bookworm and enjoys reading in her spare time. She is particularly fond of fiction and biographies, and she enjoys learning about different cultures and historical events. Earps's love of reading is evident in her social media posts, where she often recommends books to her followers.

Giving Back to the Community

Earps is passionate about giving back to the community and is involved in several charitable initiatives. She is a strong advocate for gender equality in sports and has used her platform to raise awareness of the challenges faced by women athletes.

Earps has also supported various charities that focus on education, health, and poverty alleviation. She has participated in fundraising events, visited schools, and volunteered her time to make a difference in the lives of others. Earps's commitment to social justice is an inspiration to many. She has shown that athletes can use their platform to make a positive impact on the world.

Earps's Legacy

Mary Earps

Mary Earps is a remarkable athlete who has achieved great success on and off the field. Her exceptional goalkeeping skills, her leadership qualities, and her commitment to social justice have made her a role model for many.

CHAPTER12:IMPACT AND INSPIRING THE NEXT GENERATION

Mary Earps has left a lasting legacy on women's football. Her exceptional goalkeeping skills, her leadership qualities, and her commitment to social justice have made her a role model for countless young girls and women.

Earps's journey to the top has been an inspiration to many. She has faced challenges and setbacks, but she has never given up on her dreams. Her determination, resilience, and hard work have paid off, and she has become one of the best goalkeepers in the world.

Earps's success has helped to challenge stereotypes and break down barriers in women's football. She has shown that women are capable of competing at the highest level and that they deserve to be recognized for their achievements.

Earps's commitment to social justice has also been a source of inspiration. She has used her platform to raise awareness of the challenges faced by women athletes and to call for greater investment in women's sports. Her advocacy for gender equality has helped to create a more inclusive and equitable environment for female athletes.

Earps's legacy will continue to inspire future generations of women footballers. She has shown that with hard work, dedication, and perseverance, anything is possible. Her story will continue to be told for many years to come, serving as a reminder of the incredible achievements of women in sports.

How Earps's Legacy Inspires Young Girls

Mary Earps's legacy is particularly inspiring for young girls who want to pursue their dreams in sports. She has shown them that it is possible to achieve great things, even if you come from a small town or face challenges along the way. Earps's success has also helped to normalize women's sports. Young girls can now see role models like Earps who are excelling at the highest level. This can encourage them to participate in sports and pursue their own goals.

Earps's commitment to social justice is also an inspiration to young girls. She has shown them that they can use their voices to make a difference in the world. Her advocacy for gender equality has helped to create a more inclusive and equitable environment for all.

Earps's Impact on the Future of Women's Football

Mary Earps's legacy will continue to have a positive impact on the future of women's football. She has helped to pave the way for the next generation of female athletes and has inspired countless young girls to take up the sport.

Earps's success has also helped to increase interest in women's football. More and more people are watching and following women's leagues and tournaments. This increased attention is leading to greater investment in women's sports, which will help to create more opportunities for female athletes.

Earps's commitment to social justice is also helping to create a more inclusive and equitable environment for women in sports. Her advocacy for gender equality is leading to positive change and is inspiring others to fight for equality.

CONCLUSION

As we come to the end of Mary Earps' inspiring goalkeeping journey, we are reminded of the bravery, resilience, and determination that she has displayed throughout her career. Mary's story serves as a shining example of how hard work, perseverance, and a positive attitude can lead to success on and off the soccer field. Young readers, like you, have witnessed the incredible feats and heroic saves that Mary has made, showing us the importance of courage and teamwork in achieving our goals. Just like Mary, you can tackle challenges head-on, face obstacles with determination, and never give up on your dreams, no matter how big they may seem.

As you continue your own soccer journey, remember the lessons that Mary Earps has

Mary Earps

taught us – believe in yourself, work hard, and embrace every opportunity to grow and improve. Whether you're playing in the goal or running across the field, carry Mary's spirit of resilience and courage with you, knowing that you have the power to achieve greatness just like your goalkeeping guardian.

So, young soccer enthusiasts, go forth with confidence, chase your dreams with determination, and always remember the fearless Mary Earps, the goalkeeping guardian who has shown us that anything is possible when we believe in ourselves and never stop trying. The soccer field is waiting for your skills, your passion, and your unwavering dedication. Let's go out there and make Mary proud with every save, every goal, and every moment of joy that the beautiful game brings us.

Keep kicking, keep dreaming, and keep believing in yourself – just like the incredible

Mary Earps

Mary Earps. The goal is yours to defend, the game is yours to conquer, and the world of soccer is waiting for you to write your own heroic story. Get out there, young goalkeepers and soccer fans, and let your courage and resilience shine bright on the field. The soccer ball is in your hands – make your mark and always remember the fearless spirit of the one and only Mary Earps.

Let's kick off a new adventure – are you ready to be the goalkeeping guardian of your own soccer dreams? Go for it, young champions, and embrace the magic and excitement of the beautiful game with all your heart and courage. The field is yours – let's go and conquer it together!

Made in United States
Orlando, FL
08 March 2025